PENGUIN
A DOSE OF

Rasipuram Krishnaswamy Laxman was born and educated in Mysore. Soon after he graduated from the University of Mysore, he started drawing cartoons for the *Free Press Journal*, a newspaper in Bombay. Six months later he joined the *Times of India*, a newspaper he has been with, as staff cartoonist, for over fifty years. He has written and published numerous short stories, essays and travel articles. Some of these were published in a book, *Idle Hours*. He has also written two novels, *The Hotel Riviera* and *The Messenger*, both published by Penguin Books. Penguin has also published a collection entitled *50 Years of Independence Through the Eyes of R.K. Laxman*. Laxman's autobiography, entitled *The Tunnel of Time*, was published by Penguin Books in the same month.

R.K. Laxman was awarded the prestigious Padma Bhushan by the Government of India. The University of Marathwada conferred an honorary Doctor of Literature degree on him. He has won many awards for his cartoons, including Asia's top journalism award, the Ramon Magsaysay Award, in 1984.

R.K. Laxman lives in Mumbai.

R.K. Laxman

A DOSE OF LAUGHTER

PENGUIN BOOKS

Penguin Books India (P) Ltd., 11 Community Centre, Panchsheel Park, New Delhi 110 017, India
Penguin Books Ltd., 80 Strand, London WC2R 0RL, UK
Penguin Putnam Inc., 375 Hudson Street, New York, NY 10014, USA
Penguin Books Australia Ltd., 250 Camberwell Road, Camberwell, Victoria 3124, Australia
Penguin Books Canada Ltd., 10 Alcorn Avenue, Suite 300, Toronto, Ontario, M4V 3B2, Canada
Penguin Books (NZ) Ltd., Cnr Rosedale and Airborne Roads, Albany, Auckland, New Zealand

First published by Penguin Books India 2002

Illustrations copyright © R.K. Laxman 2002

All rights reserved

10 9 8 7 6 5 4 3 2 1

Typeset in Sabon by S.R. Enterprises, New Delhi
Printed at Saurabh Print-O-Pack, Noida

This book is sold subject to the condition that it shall not, by way of trade or otherwise, be lent, resold, hired out, or otherwise circulated without the publisher's prior written consent in any form of binding or cover other than that in which it is published and without a similar condition including this condition being imposed on the subsequent purchaser and without limiting the rights under copyright reserved above, no part of this publication may be reproduced, stored in or introduced into a retrieval system, or transmitted in any form or by any means (electronic, mechanical, photocopying, recording or otherwise), without the prior written permission of both the copyright owner and the above-mentioned publisher of this book.

Publisher's Note

This book contains 100 of the funniest cartoons R.K. Laxman has drawn over the years about doctors, the medical profession, and health care in general. To complement this selection, we have added a hundred doctor-related jokes from all over the world. Together, the jokes and the cartoons will provide much-needed comic relief to physicians and their patients alike.

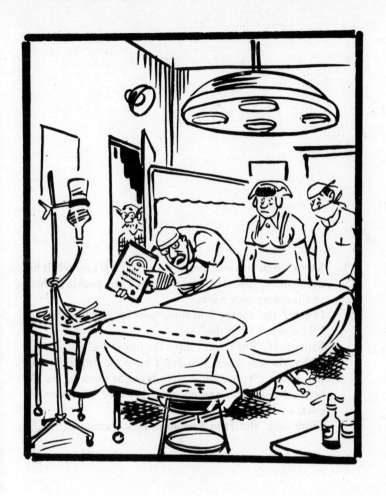

All right, have a look! Genuine degree and there was no bribing to get one in our days!

1

1. Santa Singh was working with an electric saw when he accidentally sawed off all ten fingers. He quickly rushed to the emergency room.

   'There,' the doctor told him, 'give me the fingers and I'll see what I can do.'

   Santa said, 'But I don't have the fingers!'

   'What do you mean you don't have the fingers?' said the doctor. 'You should have brought them to me. A little microsurgery and your hands would have been as good as new!'

   Santa said, 'But Doc, I couldn't pick them up.'

*I didn't want to disturb you when you were working, sir.
But it is this leg which is injured!*

3

2. A psychiatrist was testing a patient's personality. He drew a circle on a piece of paper, and asked the patient, 'What does this remind you of?'

    The patient answered, 'Sex.'

    The shrink drew a square and asked again, 'What does this remind you of?'

    'Sex,' the patient replied.

    Then the doctor drew a triangle.

    'It reminds me of sex,' the patient stated.

    'You seem to be obsessed with sex,' the shrink told the patient.

    '*I'm* obsessed with sex? *You're* the one who's drawing the dirty pictures!'

The patient sitting in this chair finds the pain more bearable when I extract the tooth.

5

3. Did you hear about the man who swears that a doctor's prescription can take you places?

He used it for two years as a railroad pass.
It got him into Radio City Music Hall twice, and once into Yankee Stadium.
It came in handy as a letter from his employer to the cashier to increase his salary.
And to top it all, his daughter played it on the piano and won a scholarship to the Curtis Music Conservatory.

This rare Himalayan herb will cure your headache. If it doesn't, I'll give you a pill prepared by a famous multinational drug house.

7

4. One afternoon, a man went to his doctor and told him that he hadn't been keeping well lately. The doctor examined the man, left the room and came back with three different bottles of pills. Then he gave the patient the following instructions: 'Take the green pill with a big glass of water when you wake up. Take the blue pill with a big glass of water after you eat lunch. Then just before going to bed, take the red pill with another big glass of water.'

Startled at being put on so many medicines, the man stammered, 'My God, Doctor, what exactly is the problem with me?'

The doctor replied solemnly, 'You're not drinking enough water.'

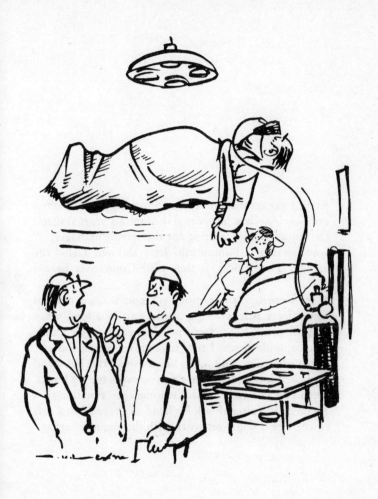

Look, young man, I clearly asked you to put him on oxygen and not hydrogen!

5. Jerry, a garage mechanic, was removing valves from a car's engine when he spotted the famous heart surgeon Dr Samuel Kaiser waiting for the service manager.

Somewhat of a loudmouth, Jerry shouted across the garage, 'Hey Kaiser, is that you? Come over here a minute.'

A bit surprised, the famous surgeon walked over to where Jerry was working on the car. In a loud voice that all could hear, Jerry proclaimed, 'So Mr Fancy Doctor, look at me. I too, take valves out, grind'em, put in new parts, and when I'm finished, this baby will purr like a kitten. How is it that you make the big bucks, when you and I are basically doing the same thing?'

To this, Dr Kaiser shook his head and replied in a soft voice, 'Try doing your work with the engine running.'

Yes, I'll be rather busy this year; a seminar to attend on cold in Manila, another one in Hawaii on cough, yet another on headache in Rio...

11

6. A man went to an eye specialist to get his eyes tested and asked, 'Doctor, will I be able to read after wearing glasses?'
    'Yes, of course,' said the doctor, 'why not?'
    'Oh! That would be great,' said the patient with great joy, 'I thought I would never learn to read.'

With the kind of money he made by adulterating life-saving drugs, he could buy his way into any place!

13

7. A psychotherapist, who had started from scratch, was having such success in his business that he could now afford to have a proper banner advertising his practice. He told a young boy to paint the signboard for him and put it above the entrance to his chamber.

He soon noticed, however, that instead of his business building up, it was beginning to slacken. It was when his assistant observed that the ladies in particular were shying away from his office after reading the signboard that he decided to check it out himself.

There at the entrance was a small wooden board that read,'PSYCHO-THE-RAPIST'!

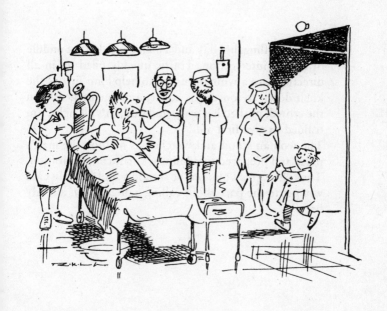

Didn't you know he is a child prodigy?

8. It was a stifling, hot day and a man fainted in the middle of a busy intersection. Traffic quickly piled up in all directions, so a woman rushed to help him. Just as she knelt down to loosen his collar, a man emerged from the crowd, pushed her aside and said, 'It's all right, I'm trained to give first aid.'

    The woman stood and watched as he took the man's pulse and prepared to administer artificial respiration. Then she tapped him on the shoulder and said, 'In case you get to the part about calling a doctor, I'm already here.'

...they can fix anything these days, kidney, heart, bone, eyes, hair—actually I myself am 96% transplant!

9. Four psychiatrists met up at a convention.
    One of them said, 'People always come to us with their
    guilt and fears, but we have no one that we can go to
    when we have problems.'
    Then another suggested, 'Since we are all professionals,
    why don't we take some time right now to hear each
    other out?'
    The other three agreed heartily.
    The first psychiatrist said, 'I have an uncontrollable
    desire to kill my patients.'
    The second psychiatrist said, 'I love expensive things.
    So I find ways to cheat my patients out of their money
    whenever I can to buy the things I want.'
    The third followed with, 'I sell drugs and often get my
    patients to sell them for me.'
    The fourth psychiatrist then confessed, 'I know I'm not
    supposed to, but no matter how hard I try, I can't keep
    a secret.'

I thought you were a good doctor—so that's what you are up to when we are on strike.

10. A man walked into the psychiatrist's office looking devastated.

    'Doctor,' he said, 'I'm so depressed and lonely. I don't have any friends, no one will come near me, and everybody laughs at me. Can you help me accept my ugliness?'

    'Of course I can,' the psychiatrist replied. 'Just go over and lie face down on that couch.'

It became so frequent, the authorities decided finally to give
it a permanent position.

11. A doctor in a mental hospital on his morning rounds entered one of the rooms.

    He found Patient #1 sitting on the floor, pretending to saw a piece of wood in half, while Patient #2 was hanging from the ceiling by his feet.

    The doctor asked Patient #1 what he was doing. The patient replied, 'Can't you see I'm sawing this piece of wood in half?'

    The doctor then asked Patient #1 what Patient #2 was doing. Patient #1 replied, 'Oh he's my friend, but he's a little crazy. He thinks he's a light bulb.'

    The doctor looked up and noticed tha Patient #2's face was turning red.

    The doctor asked Patient #1, 'If he's your friend, you should get him down from there before he hurts himself.'

    Patient #1 replied, 'What? And work in the dark?'

The resident doctors are still on strike. So we are utilizing the services of every type of medical practitioner.

12. Patient: What are the chances of my recovery doctor?
    Doctor: One hundred per cent. Medical records show
    that nine out of ten people die of the disease you have.
    Yours is the tenth case I've treated. All the others died.

Eureka! I've discovered it—a way to emigrate!

13. A young mother paying a visit to a doctor made no attempt to restrain her five-year-old son, who was ransacking an adjoining room.

Finally, a rather loud clatter of bottles prompted her to say, 'I hope you don't mind my son being in there.'

'Not at all,' said the doctor calmly, 'he'll become quiet when he gets to the poison.'

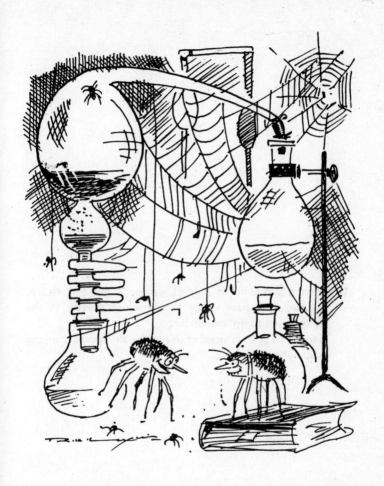

The nice thing about this research lab is that the scientists here are all the time out attending seminars, leaving you completely undisturbed!

14. Patient: Whenever I drink coffee, I get this sharp, excruciating pain in my throat which travels all the way down to my stomach.
Doctor: Try to remember to remove the spoon from the cup before drinking.

Thanks Doctor, I am able to see far better now.

15. Vivek: It's been one month since my last visit to you and I still feel miserable.
Dr Mallik: Did you follow the instructions on the bottle of medicine I gave you?
Vivek: I sure did. The bottle said 'Keep Tightly Closed'.

I ruined his work of a lifetime! Instead of rushing towards the food when he rang the bell I ran in the opposite direction, deliberately!

16. Patient: Doctor, Doctor, I think I am a cat!
    Doctor: How long has this been going on?
    Patient: Oh, since I was a kitten I guess!

I'm worried he is not like other kids. I want to show him to a psychiatrist.

17. Sardarji: Doctor, I have a problem.
    Doctor: What's your problem?
    Sardarji: I keep forgetting things.
    Doctor: Since when have you had this problem?
    Sardarji: What problem?

We are lucky. We are in a civilized desert!

18. Patient: Doctor, can you give me something for my hands—they shake all the time.
Doctor: Do you drink a lot?
Patient: Well, I wish I could, but I seem to spill most of it!

Conditions are excellent here, young man—he was brought here for experimental purposes and today he heads the department!

37

19. A patient was waiting nervously in the examination room of a famous specialist.

'So who did you see before coming to me?' asked the doctor.

'The local general practitioner.'

'Your GP?' scoffed the doctor. 'What a complete waste of time. Tell me, what sort of useless advice did he give you?'

'He told me to come and see you.'

That one, madam, is for ladies. It always shows 20 kg less.

20. After completing a patient's treatment, the dentist pleaded, 'Could you help me? Could you give out a few of your loudest, most painful screams?'

'Why Doctor?' the surprised patient queried. 'It wasn't all that bad this time.'

Nodding apologetically the dentist replied, 'There are too many people in the waiting room right now, and I don't want to miss the four o'clock soccer match.'

No thanks! I just had one at the previous mirage!

21. A dentist asks a patient while poking inside his mouth with a pointed instrument: Tell me if it hurts.
The patient replies: And while I'm telling you, you tell me if I bite.

Remember the test-tube baby? We had to keep on increasing the size of the test-tube—he refuses to step out.

22. A man goes to the dentist and says: My teeth are kind of yellow, what do you recommend?
With supreme confidence the dentist replies: A brown tie!

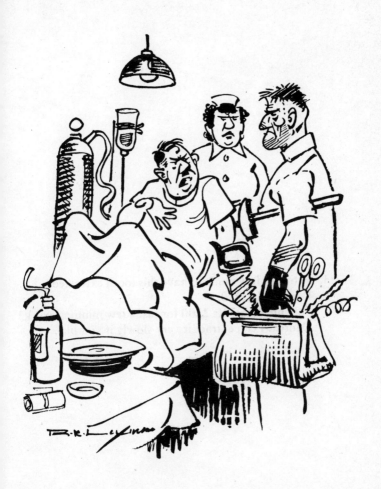

Let me see your medical degree, please, before you start operating.

23. Patient: How much to have this tooth extracted?
    Dentist: Rs 2200.
    Patient: What? Rs 2200 for just a few minutes' work?
    Dentist: I can extract it very slowly if you like.

Wipe off that I-told-you-so look!

24. An artist asked the gallery owner if there had been any interest in his paintings on display at that time.

'I have good news and bad news,' the owner replied. 'The good news is that a gentleman inquired about your work and wondered if its value would increase after your death. When I told him it would, he bought all fifteen of your paintings.'

'That's wonderful,' the artist exclaimed. 'What's the bad news?'

'The guy was your doctor.'

What a waste of time! When you kept saying 'Can't read, can't read', I didn't realize you didn't go to school!

25. 'Open wider,' requested the dentist, as he began
    examining the patient.
    'Good God!' he said, startled. 'You've got the biggest
    cavity I've ever seen—the biggest cavity I've ever seen.'
    'Ok Doctor!' replied the patient. 'I'm scared enough
    without you saying something like that twice.'
    'I didn't,' said the dentist. 'That was the echo!'

I picked up the habit in the research lab I escaped from.
They were testing the bad effects of smoking on me.

26. A business executive on an adventure holiday injured his leg while trekking up a hill. By the time he got home, his leg had swollen up and he was finding it difficult to walk. So he called his physician.

The doctor told him to soak his leg in hot water. But after he had soaked it in hot water for some time, the leg became more swollen and painful.

His maid saw him limping and said, 'I don't know, I'm only a maid, but I always thought it was better to use cold water, not hot water, for a swelling.' So he switched to cold water, and the swelling subsided rapidly.

On Sunday afternoon he called his doctor again; this time, to complain. 'What kind of a doctor are you anyway? You told me to soak my leg in hot water, and it got worse. My maid told me to use cold water and it got better.'

'Really?' answered the doctor. 'But I don't understand it; my maid was quite confident that hot water did the trick.'

Don't complain about backache, giddiness, debility. Remember, you should have been extinct millions of years ago!

27. Mohan was new to the city and was suffering from a
    recurring backache. 'I need to see a doctor,' he told his
    colleague Rakesh. 'Can you recommend a good one?'
    'You should go to Dr Sethi,' said Rakesh.
    'He's good, is he?'
    'Well, half his patients swear by him.'
    'What about the other half?' asked Mohan, intrigued.
    'They swear AT him.'

*I asked you to get an enlarged picture of the isolated virus
and not the real one enlarged!*

28. A doctor answers his phone and hears a colleague's voice at the other end of the line saying, 'We need a fourth for a game of bridge.'

'I'll be right over,' whispers the doctor.

As he is putting on his coat, his wife asks, 'Is it serious?'

'Oh yes, quite serious,' says the doctor gravely. 'In fact, there are three doctors there already!'

Why do you want me to resign on health grounds? Why not on moral grounds like so many others?

29. The dentist looked into his patient's mouth and said, 'The only way I can cure your bad breath is by taking out all your teeth.'

'Will I be able to sing in the choir for the Independence Day function?' asked the patient.

'I don't see why not,' replied the dentist.

'Well, I wasn't good enough to sing in it the last time I auditioned.'

And that is my mother—I'm a test-tube baby.

30. A pipe burst in a doctor's house and a plumber was sent for.

The plumber arrived, unpacked his tools, rattled around for a while, and handed the doctor a bill for Rs 3000.

The doctor exclaimed, 'This is ridiculous! I don't make that much even as a doctor!'

The plumber waited for him to finish and quietly said, 'Neither did I when I was a doctor.'

Nothing really wrong. The strain of the bold front he is putting on in public these days is telling on him.

31. A doctor had been attending to a rich old man for some time, but it soon became apparent that the old chap did not have long to live.

Accordingly, the doctor advised his wealthy patient to put his affairs in order.

'Oh yes, I've done that already,' said the old gentleman. 'I've only got to make a will.

And do you know what I'm going to do with all my money? I'm going to leave it to the doctor who saves my life.'

Don't feel bad. These days, if you are in politics in a sovereign democratic republic like ours, this is bound to happen.

32. Doctor: I'm afraid I've got bad news for you. You've only got five minutes to live.
Patient: But Doctor, isn't there anything you can do for me?
Doctor (after some thought): Well, I could boil you an egg.

Be careful about what you eat! There are quite a few cases of poisoning around, I understand!

33. Vishal: Why are you so upset?
    Vicky: My wife introduced me to her psychiatrist this morning.
    Vishal: Well, what's wrong with that?
    Vicky: She said to him, 'Doctor, this is my husband. You know, one of the men I've been telling you about.'

*Very bad! I didn't know you were an MP fighting for secular
values, minority rights, political ethics...*

34. A man who was visiting the doctor for his annual physical check-up was looking rather worried. When the doctor asked him whether anything was troubling him, he said, 'Well, to tell you the truth, yes. You see, I seem to be getting quite forgetful. I'm never sure where I park the car, or whether I've answered a letter, or where I'm going, or what it is I'm going to do once I get there—if I get there at all. I really need your help. What should I do?'

The doctor thought for a moment, and then answered, 'Please pay me in advance.'

I don't think exposed food is harmful any more! The city has become so filthy. I am sure no fly or bacteria has survived!

35. Doctor: You seem to be in excellent health, Mr Seth.
Your pulse is as steady and regular as clockwork.
Mr Seth: That's because your fingers are on my watch.

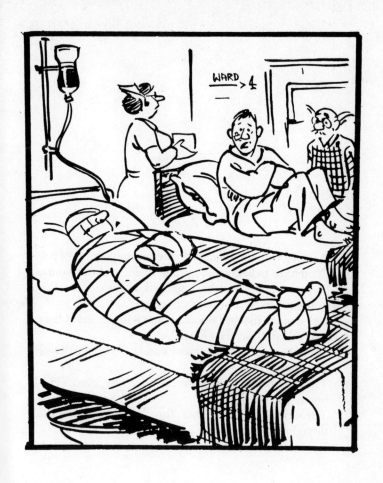

I was lucky, I was beaten up only by gangsters. But that innocent man was beaten up by the VIP's security police!

36. A young woman went to her doctor complaining of pain. 'You have to help me, I hurt all over,' said the woman. 'Where exactly is it hurting?' asked the doctor. 'You will have to be a little more specific.'

The woman touched her right knee with her index finger and yelled, 'Ow, that hurts.'

Then she touched her left cheek and yelled again, 'Ouch! That hurts, too.'

Then she touched her right earlobe, 'Ow, even THAT hurts,' she cried.

The doctor checked her for a moment and said thoughtfully, 'You have a broken finger.'

Body pain, leg ache, sore throat. Sometimes I feel like defecting to the ruling party!

37. Psychiatrist: Well, what's your problem?
    Patient: I prefer brown shoes to black shoes.
    Psychiatrist: There's nothing wrong with that? Many
    people prefer brown shoes to black shoes. I do so myself.
    Patient: Really? And how do you like yours—fried or
    boiled?

Get an aircraft ready. I must make an aerial survey of the affected areas!

38. A noted psychiatrist was a guest at a chic gathering, and his hostess naturally broached the subject in which he was most at ease.

'Would you mind telling me, Doctor,' she asked, 'how you detect a mental deficiency in somebody who appears to be absolutely normal?'

'Nothing is easier,' he replied. 'You ask him a simple question which everyone should answer with no trouble. If he hesitates you know he requires help.'

'What sort of question?' the hostess asked intrigued.

'Well,' the doctor said, 'you might ask him, "Captain Cook made three trips around the world and died during one of them. Which one?"'

The hostess looked blank for a moment and then said with a nervous laugh, 'You wouldn't happen to have another example would you? I must confess I don't know much about history.'

Sheer exhaustion due to doing things he isn't use ~~d to, taking~~ *a firm stand, making quick decisions and* ~~exercising out~~ *power...*

39. Doctor: You need spectacles.
    Patient: How did you know that without even examining
    my eyes?
    Doctor: I could tell as soon as you walked in through
    the window.

That was just to inaugurate the 'Keep the City Clean'
campaign. I don't think he will do it regularly.

40. Rajan went to Shanghai. He fell ill so he called up the hotel manager and asked if he knew the best doctor of the city. The manager said, 'If you want my advice it's Doctor Xu who is the best.'

When Rajan asked him why, he explained, 'You see, once I got wet in the rain. I started sneezing so I rushed to Doctor Su. After his treatment I got the cough. Then I was rushed to Doctor Cu whose pills did not work either and the cough turned into a severe fever. Then I was sent to Doctor Fu and it became acute hyperthermia. After that I was sent to Doctor Hu; his treatment made it pneumonia. At last my family took me to Doctor Xu. They said he was out of town and my life was saved.'

Some inner-party argument, that's all. Luckily no damage to party unity!

41. Rahul: I keep seeing spots in front of my eyes.
    Arjun: Have you ever seen a doctor?
    Rahul: No, just spots.

Don't think we are heartless. True, I beat you up mercilessly.
But then I'm rushing you to the hospital, too! Think of that!

42. Two psychiatrists were at a convention. As they conversed over a drink, one asked, 'What has been your most difficult case so far?'

The other replied, 'I had a patient who lived in a fantasy world. He believed that an uncle in South America was going to die and leave him a fortune. All day long he waited for a letter to arrive from an attorney. He never went out, he never did anything. He just sat around and waited for this fantasy letter from this fantasy uncle. I worked with this man for eight years.'

'What happened?' the first doctor asked with growing interest.

'It was one long struggle every day for eight years, but I finally cured him. And then that stupid letter arrived!'

He is that pop singer. He broke his hip bone, dislocated his shoulders, sprained his ankle when practising his new number!

43. An old woman called the hospital and asked to speak
     with the person who gives patient information. When
     the person came on the line, she said, 'I'd like to know
     about Rita Kohli, in Room 302.'

     He said, 'Kohli. Kohli. Let me see. Oh yes. Mrs Kohli
     is doing very well. In fact, she's had two full meals, her
     blood pressure is fine, and if she continues this way, her
     doctor is going to send her home on Tuesday at noon.'

     The woman said, 'Thank God! That's wonderful! She's
     going home at noon on Tuesday! I'm so happy to hear
     that. That's great news!'

     The person on the other end answered, 'From your
     enthusiasm I take it you must be a close family
     member.'

     She said, 'Close? I'll say! I am Rita Kohli! But my doctor
     doesn't tell me anything!'

The situation is normal. All tests have proved negative—no plague, only malaria, jaundice, typhoid, cholera, dengue...

44. The doctor took his patient into the room and said, 'I have some good news and some bad news.'
The patient said, 'Give me the good news first.'
'They're going to name the disease after you.'

You must congratulate your staff. The situation has been brought back to normal—not a single death due to plague.

45. How many surgeons does it take to change a light bulb?

   None. They would wait for a suitable donor and do a filament transplant.

The general ward is over there. You see this is purely for crew members who, having so many demands to make frequently, have to report sick.

46. 'The doctor said he would have me on my feet in two weeks.'
'And did he?'
'Yes, I had to sell the car to pay his bill.'

I've got it! I have at last taught the antibodies karate!

47. Patient: Doctor, Doctor, I keep thinking I am a set of curtains!
Doctor: Pull yourself together man!

That's our crisis manager!

48. Patient: Doctor, Doctor, I keep thinking I'm a bell.
Doctor: Well, just go home and if the feeling persists,
give me a ring.

*All the tests show that he genuinely has a cardiac condition.
Probably because he is innocent really!*

49. Patient: Doctor, Doctor, I've only got fifty-nine seconds to live.
    Doctor: Please wait for a minute.

What's going on? He is the seventeenth one to say he's sorry but he has a backache and can't bend to touch my feet!

50. Patient: Doctor, Doctor, I keep thinking I'm invisible.
    Doctor: Who said that?

Your liver, heart, lungs, kidneys, blood pressure and blood sugar are all fine. I recommend you consult a high-powered lawyer.

101

51. Patient: Doctor, Doctor, people keep ignoring me!
    Doctor: Next!

Why have we come this way to go to the hospital just next door? The other roads are blocked because of the VIP movement!

52. Patient: Doctor, Doctor, no one believes a word I say.
Doctor: Tell me the truth now; what's your REAL
problem?

Here, drop all that. It's about your immediate transfer to the department of rural health and sanitation.

53. Riaz went to the doctor for a check-up and was just stepping out of his clothes when he noticed the doctor rummaging through his wallet.

Enraged at the sight, he said accusingly, 'What do you think you're doing, Doctor? Do you have no ethics?'

The doctor looked at him quite calmly and replied, 'But I thought you wanted a "complete" check-up.'

He has done it ten times already! It's to get bail on medical grounds, I think.

54. Aditi bumped into her school friend Reema at the neighbourhood book store. They hadn't met in several years and Aditi had got married in the meantime. 'And how is married life treating you?' asked Reema.

'Oh, fine,' said Aditi.

'What does your husband do?'

'He's a doctor.'

'Where did you...how did you...I mean...'

'I had the flu.'

'I—don't think I got you.'

'See—he was the neighbourhood GP. I kept asking him to make a house call, and he refused to turn up. Then I figured that the only way to get a doctor to make a house call was to marry him. So here we are.'

Could be a case of slipped disc, sir! They wouldn't have minded really if you hadn't joined them!

55. Nisha was fuming when she returned from her doctor's appointment. 'I'm never going back there,' she growled.

'Whatever happened?' her husband asked.

'I'm changing doctors, and that's final,' she scowled.

'What did he do?' asked her husband anxiously.

'It's his chamber—there's no television in the waiting room and I missed my favourite soap.'

But, in my opinion, this one is clearly a case of language issue and that a case of demand for statehood!

56. Dr Khan was on his way to the hospital when a middle-aged man suddenly came up to him and said very sincerely, 'Thank you Doctor. I will never forget what you have done for me.'

Quite overwhelmed, but still confused the doctor told him, 'I am sorry but I don't recall what it is that I have cured you of.'

'From all my worries Doc,' the man replied, 'you sent my wife away for a rest cure.'

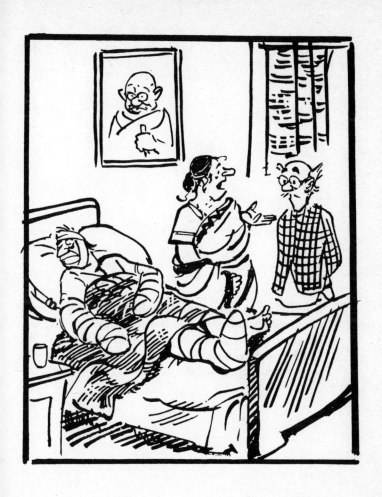

He is so obstinate! I begged and pleaded with him not to visit his constituency!

57. A well-known practitioner finally found time to call on an elderly lady who had been frantically calling his chamber. As he entered the house he heard her say: 'Oh Doc I thought you would never arrive and I would have to die without your help!'

If you are feeling tired why don't you go home and rest after the pandemonium and rushing to the well?

58. A doctor had been treating a patient with severe pharyngitis for well over a month.

Finally one day he found the patient's condition improving.

'Well your cough seems to be improving,' he said to the patient encouragingly.

'I thought so Doctor,' he replied. 'After all I was practising all night.'

Something fishy, sir! He is complaining of blackouts, uneasiness, chest pains and yet he swears he is not a business tycoon or ex-minister!

59. Two men sat discussing life and its little ironies over a drink.

    'You're telling me,' said one to the other. 'I sacrificed everything so that my son could become a doctor, and now he tells me that I have to quit smoking.'

He was telling me about the bold and tough decisions he was going to take. Then suddenly he trembled and fainted!

60. At the crossroads of their lives, a few friends sat on their school porch discussing where life would take them. While most of them seemed unsure about what they wanted to do, Gaurav declared that he had already made up his mind to become a doctor.

'How the hell are you so sure?' his friends questioned.

'Are you kidding?' he said. 'A doctor is the only man who can tell a woman to take off all her clothes and then send her husband a bill for it!'

He had breathing trouble during the taxi strike. The doctor said he wasn't used to pollution-free air, that's why.

61. On his first day in the hospital as a doctor, Kevin was asked to check on a patient. As his supervisor looked on, Kevin held her wrist and slowly shook his head. Finally with a sigh he told her, 'Sorry there's nothing I can do for you.'

When the patient left, the supervisor asked Kevin, 'And you recognized the seriousness of her condition just by checking her pulse?'

'No sir,' replied Kevin. 'I had already had a feel of her purse.'

It went off very well, thank you, except that he didn't see the flowerpot near his feet...

62. 'I had the strangest experience today,' said Dr Rajan, a psychiatrist, to a fellow colleague. 'This guy entered my chamber, and when I asked him to lie down on the couch, he crawled under it.'

'Oh,' his colleague said with a smile, 'was it the auto mechanic from down the street?'

Ah, removed it! But this is happening once too often. I would advise you to resign from politics.

63. Nalini came back from her visit to the psychiatrist bursting with rage.
'I can't believe that doctor's audacity,' she screamed.
Worried, her husband asked her what the doctor had done.
'I don't know what gave him the idea that he could meddle in my private life.'

The analysis shows that your boy definitely has certain criminal tendencies.

64. 'I don't believe this!' Ajit cried, tearing open a letter that had come by the morning's post.
'What is it?' asked his wife.
'My psychiatrist has charged me a double fee.'
'Why would he do that?'
'Well, he did say I have a split personality.'

Listen, about the protest bandh you organized, it says, 'It went off peacefully without any untoward incidents...'

65. A postman entered a nudist camp to deliver a letter.
    'I'm looking for Dr Smith, the psychiatrist,' he said to
    one of the guests.
    'There he is now,' said the guest, pointing to a far corner.
    'He's the one who's listening instead of looking.'

*What's your complaint now? The doctor advised me to go
on a holiday and relax—and I am on a holiday relaxing!*

66. 'I've decided to change my psychiatrist,' declared Peter to his parents.

'Why? What's the matter?' inquired his father.

'He's just too busy,' Peter sulked.

'So are most doctors,' his father said trying to pacify him.

'I know, but mine has a couch with an upper and a lower berth.'

I have invented a miracle cure for a disease that is yet to be discovered, Doctor!

67. A recent survey of the number of people requiring treatment for mental disorders has resulted in the following conclusion:
Three out of five people go to psychiatrists. The other two are psychiatrists.

The nice thing is that nobody here is suffering from any disease. All are healthy cases of injury in political infighting, political rivalry, political clashes...

68. Meera returned home to find her husband beating his head against the wall.
'Stop! Stop!' she cried. 'What is the matter with you?'
'You won't believe this,' he groaned. 'I just discovered that the psychiatrist I was consulting all these years has been deaf since birth!'

He must have complete rest: strict doctor's orders, no visitors—except party secretaries, ministers, MPs, VIPs, CMs, etc.

69. A man plagued by paranoia had been visiting psychiatrists since his youth. A friend who met him after a good many years noticed a subtle change in him, but couldn't figure out what it was.

'There's something different about you,' he said, squinting his eyes.

'Oh yes, of course there is. I found a great psychiatrist. He's managed to lump all my nagging little worries into one big complex.'

I analysed the loaf, sir. It is not adulterated. It's pure sawdust!

70. A doctor tells his colleague, 'Have you tried the new miracle drugs? They are absolutely marvellous.'
Excited at the prospect, his colleague asks, 'A hundred per cent success rate is it?'
'Oh yes, all the patients I've used it on have stayed alive long enough to pay their bills.'

No, sir, this famine has not affected us. We have always starved here, you see.

71. A spaceship landed on earth and the commander sent out his little green men to investigate the creatures that humans referred to as 'doctors'.

A few days later the aliens reported back to the spaceship.

'So, what do you think?' asked the commander.

'From our study of the activities of the specimens called "Doctors",' they declared, 'this is our conclusion: Most doctors pour drugs of which they know little, to cure diseases of which they know less, into human beings of whom they know nothing.'

I only read out that the police have seized the books and records of a big business firm.

72. A man was having a particularly bad day. It had started
    to rain as he left his house and he was drenched even
    before he reached the bus stop. This was followed by a
    suffocating journey in an overcrowded bus. When he
    finally got off at his stop, he discovered that his wallet
    had been stolen. After office as he was returning home
    he was mugged, stripped of his watch, jacket and shirt,
    and beaten badly.

    Somehow he managed to make his way to the hospital.
    The doctor on duty at the emergency ward looked
    shocked at his condition and asked in a concerned voice,
    'Sir, has anyone taken your pulse?'

    To which the man replied wearily, 'No, Doc. I think I
    still have that.'

I must be close to the common people, live like them, eat what they eat—he said, and was away just for a day, Doctor!

73. Tommy fell down from his cycle and bruised his knees and right elbow. Seeing him with so many bandages at school the next day, his teacher inquired, 'My God, Tommy! What happened to you? Did the doctor treat you yesterday?'

'No,' said Tommy pulling a long face, 'he charged me ten dollars.'

It's like in our movies—sex and violence!

74. One of the first patients to arrive at the doctor's chamber was an elderly lady.

Seeing that the doctor was going to be late, the nurse decided to give the lady some company.

'Hello,' she said, approaching the lady, 'I'm the doctor's nurse.'

Squinting her eyes to look up at the nurse, the lady queried, 'Oh, is the doctor sick?'

Unless he is given some good tonic soon he will never be able to go to school!

75. Deepak called up his doctor to find out the results of the recent tests that had been conducted on him.

'Well, Dr Munshi,' he said. 'How do I stand?'

'I don't know,' replied the doctor, sounding confused. 'It's quite a miracle.'

This is the trouble with having tainted politicians here! They start holding party meetings.

76. A doctor was having an affair with a patient's wife. One day the patient rang up sounding frantic. 'Doctor, I feel like killing myself,' he said. 'What shall I do?' Without realizing it, the doctor blurted out, 'Just leave that to me.'

That's right, it was a prison once. But of late every inmate started to complain about chest pains. So it was converted into a hospital.

77. Hiren's wife found him at 2.00 a.m. in the drawing room, rocking sleepily from one foot to the other with his eyes closed and the phone pressed against his ear.
'What are you doing?' she exclaimed, shaking him awake.
'I called the doctor to complain that I couldn't sleep. Now he's singing me a lullaby.'

I still think you should have told him how young you wanted to look!

78. Doctor: The tests show that you are a kleptomaniac.
Rakhi: What do you suggest I take for it?

I know, sir, I should have brought him on the stretcher—but there's such a shortage of hands!

79. Priya found her uncle jumping up and down on the terrace with great vigour.

'What's the matter, uncle?' she asked surprised at the sudden display of energy.

'The doctor forgot to shake the bottle before he gave me my medicine.'

Luckily the city is free from typhoid, dengue, malaria, etc.
Here are all the victims of shoot-outs, stone-throwing,
stabbing...

80. Having recovered from a serious illness, Nikhil had gone for a final check-up to the doctor.

Smiling brightly the doctor said, 'Young man, you owe your fine recovery to your wife's tender care.'

With a twinkle in his eyes Nikhil replied, 'Thanks Doctor. I'll make out the cheque to my wife.'

Very kind of you to offer...but people will say it's for health reasons if you do it, and not for our cause. So let him undertake the fast...

81. Dr Worah was attending to Mrs Sen when he overheard her maids talking about the old lady.

    'Did you know that the old fool has left all her money to Dr Worah?' said one maid to the other.

    As he was about to leave the house Mrs Sen asked the doctor, 'Doctor, do you think I'll live?'

    'Yes,' said the doctor, 'but I don't advise it.'

*Boil this thousand-year-old Himalayan herb in milk mixed
with lotus petals twenty times and drink it for seven months.
If all this doesn't cure you, take a couple of aspirins.*

82. Sreela: I have no idea what I'm supposed to do. Every doctor I go to seems to have a different opinion about my illness.
Aditi: You should consult my doctor immediately. I can assure you, you will never live to regret it.

Remember, the blood donated by that movie star, Doctor?
Well, it's pure tomato ketchup!

83. A vagabond shuffled into Dr Frank's chamber.
Wary of people who demanded free check-ups, the
doctor immediately shouted out, 'I will only examine
you for Rs 10.'
'Go ahead,' the old man shot back. 'If you find it, you
can have it.'

He is from the International Pollution Control Authority.
He came to check the condition of our factory.

84. Mr Brown was having an affair behind his wife's back. One night he suffered a heart attack and had to be rushed to hospital.

At the emergency ward, the doctor inquired of Mrs Brown, 'Does your husband exercise?'

'Oh yes Doctor,' she said tearfully. 'In fact, just last week he was out four nights running.'

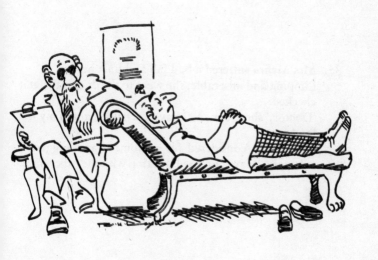

This obsession seizes you frequently—that you want to enter politics and become the PM, right? That's normal. Anything else?

85. Mrs Mehra suffered a bad fall and hurt her leg.
Limping and miserable, she went to the doctor to get it
checked.

'Doctor,' she groaned, 'I have a terrible pain in my left
leg.'

The doctor considered for a moment and suggested
solemnly, 'Have you tried walking with the other one?'

The head injury was in campaign violence, the hand in poll violence, leg in just violence!

86. The surgeon left the operation theatre looking relieved. A nurse who was passing by asked him, 'The operation was just in the nick of time, wasn't it?'
'Oh yes,' the surgeon replied, 'he would have recovered in another ten hours.'

Very brave of you, young man, to have hit a police officer and run away. You are under arrest, I happen to be that officer!

87. Son: Daddy, why do you wear a mask in the operation theatre?
    Father: Well son, I need to make sure no one identifies me if something goes wrong.

*No, he won't lie down. He says he is feeling fine and is not
hurt all that badly!*

88. Mita called Veena and whispered conspiratorially, 'Did you know that Seema's husband has been hospitalized?' 'What! How is that possible?' cried Veena. 'Just yesterday I saw him with a pretty, young girl.' 'Aha! And so did Seema!'

He tried everything for his backache. With this new treatment he says he sleeps soundly!

89. Anita: Hey! What are you doing back home? I thought you were to be in hospital for another two days.
Neha: I couldn't stay there any more. It was a weird place—they woke me up at 3 a.m. to give me sleeping pills.

A message from the Centre, sir! It says you are keeping indifferent health and that you want to resign and step down before noon tomorrow, sir.

90. Two friends were discussing their doctors.

'My doctor has the latest medical test facilities right there in his office, so I don't have to run around collecting reports from ten thousand places,' boasted Amit.

'Well, my doctor uses the shock treatment to cure anything I complain about,' said Hari.

'How does that work?' asked Amit curiously.

'He just sends me the bill in advance.'

Let him go—no use holding down anyone who is unwilling to work here and wants to emigrate!

91. After a particularly bad fall down the stairs, Kunal whined to the doctor, 'Please do something Doctor. Every bone in my body aches.'
'What are you complaining about?' said the doctor. 'You should be glad you're not a herring.'

Ah, with this I can see clearly! Again from the top, A, B, C, D, E, F, G...

92. A notoriously mischievous student in medical college was up to his usual tricks.

'How long can a man survive without a brain, sir?' he asked a professor innocently.

This time, the professor was ready for him. He promptly replied, 'I don't know really,' then added after a pause, 'how old are *you*?'

I have produced, at last, the test-tube robot!

93. Nita saw her friend Simi hurrying along the road.
'Where are you running off to?' she inquired.
Panting, Simi replied, 'I'm on my way to the cardiologist.'
'I hope it's nothing serious,' said Nita.
'Of course it is,' was the reply. 'I just received the bill from another doctor who treated me for a cold.'

No, no, son, you will fall sick if you eat this exposed food!

94. Did you hear of the doctor who became a kidnapper and failed miserably at it?

Nobody could read the ransom notes he wrote.

It's water, all right. But I wouldn't drink it if I were you. It's not boiled or filtered!

95. After checking a patient's throat, the doctor told her husband, 'Well, clearly it's a case of laryngitis.'
The husband leaned forward and whispered in his ears, 'Doctor, what can you give her that will clear it up in a month or two?'

He used to work in our lab before. He's retired now!

96. Two months had passed and a patient had still not payed
the doctor's bills.

Losing patience, the doctor called up the man to demand
the payment.

'But Doc,' said the patient mournfully, 'I can't pay your
bills.'

'What?' exclaimed the doctor. 'Why ever not?'

'Well, you asked me to slow down. I did, and I lost my
job.'

Can't unwind, is it? I told you not to follow books written by quacks.

97. Pavan's grandfather took one look at the doctor's diagnosis of his ailment and stated grimly, 'Medical science has indeed made great progress in the past generation.'

As Pavan looked on expecting a revelation, Grandad elaborated, 'What used to be an itch, is now an allergy.'

Taking medicines all the time! He had always been a hypochondriac!

98. A patient on her first visit to the doctor spent over an hour in his chamber. After she left, the doctor came out of his chamber shaking his head and inhaling deeply. The receptionist exclaimed, 'Wow, that was some marathon visit.'
The doctor replied, 'No, that was a preamble to her constitution.'

He just sent word he won't be coming; he had to rush to yet another international conference of surgeons!

99. A particularly sour-tempered nurse was harassing Rajeev during his week-long stay in hospital.

An old aunt came to visit him and remarked in all her wisdom, 'I always told you, an apple a day keeps the doctor away.'

Rajeev promptly replied, 'And what does it take to get rid of the nurse?'

*He was rushed in only yesterday and now is rushing out!
You can't blame the poor fellow, the conditions here are so
bad!*

199

100. Ravi: Doctor, I suffer from severe insomnia. I lie awake all night staring into space.
Doctor (after some thought): Why don't you go and sleep it off? Everything will be all right in the morning.